Everlasting Change

Laura Chambers

BookLeaf Publishing

Presentation by *BookLeaf Publishing*

Web: www.bookleafpub.com

E-mail: info@bookleafpub.com

ISBN: 9789395890243

First edition 2023

Peace on the waters

Catch my breath, see the waters hit the bay, I stand there looking over, in my mind no say. Peace surrounds the rocks, presence swims around. Each wave pushing, till I find the light, that was once lost but now found. No voice to be heard, once you stand places that are always there but not today no word. Remember this moment, cherish it forever, come back another time, feel this peace, time stands still, it's time that's never.

Over the horizon

Protected and young, love to build the strength through hardship, once had begun. Blue waters brighten the surfaces, stars blind the horizon. Take my hand, grow your wings, take my place, more chases. Find your way, each step you take, our bond will never break. I see this I believe; belief is given through seeing the brightness.

Hypnotised crystal waters

Hypnotised by you, rippling away fast or slow, no noise nor movement surrounding me, I shall not go. Blue crystal waters waving through the sand, aggressive yet peaceful, wanting to remain in this place, reality taking this away, lock memory. Remember its face.

Staircase

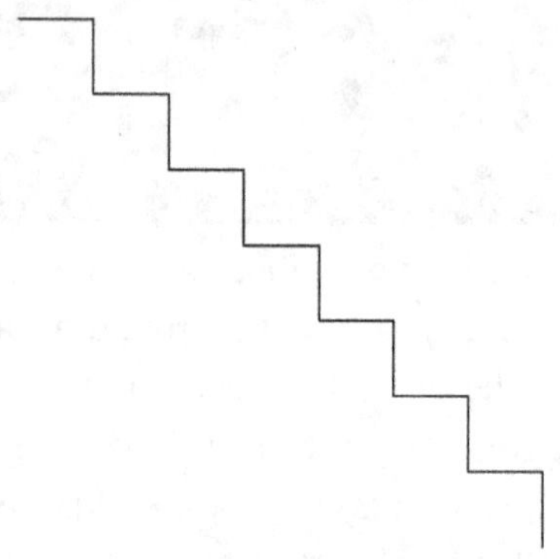

Stuck on the staircase blocked by barricaded doors, no one there to open them up, except you, you showed me more. The nerves on not being able to trust, showing me comfort and love, maybe there's a must. The world is bigger than these steps, scary yet beautiful, hold my hand, I don't want to be alone behind this wall. You say look at the stars, they're the light in the dark, you say I'm your light in your dark, I hope these moments last, don't extinguish this spark. Believe in yourself before believing the thoughts that make you think otherwise, I won't be taken back to those stairs, you held me away, you helped me rise.

Real nightmares

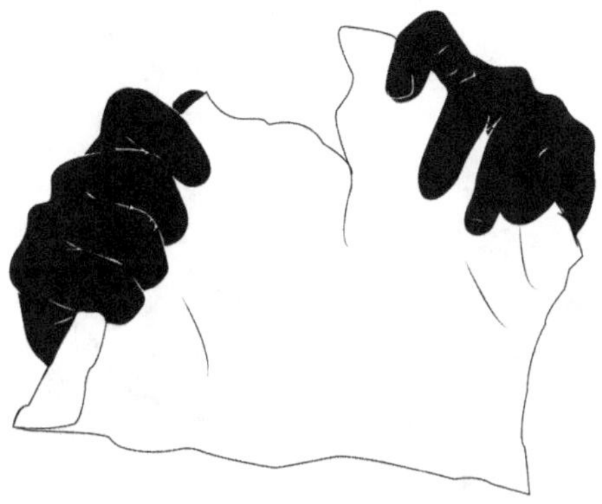

You hurt me, still hurt me. Always on my mind haunting me, not letting me free. Pin me down in the nightmares, put asleep in the dream, check myself for change, something happened it seems. Upon touch from others afraid, cry over the pain as I lay. See your face there, I shiver. Hearing your name, I enrage, but why I tell myself, these blocked memories are there locked in a cage. Forget they say, I try, everything in there it's real nor a lie.

Hollow mind

Hollow mind, tears arising, emotion left. Pain came, surprise! Robbing you again, no rest just theft. Explain, enter my home, see if you can tell the story, I sure can't, most rooms locked, few left open, ones stayed closed, hear no rant, just see me coping. Take a break, you're obsessed, you're my stalker, hovering over me, I feel your breath. Let myself back, open my house up, let her in, she's better than you, I won't let you win.

Electric lies

Different, what a word, used-good or bad, throw away my power with your electric lies. Pushed away, outcasted through this gate, under you, I'm more above than you, my hands all ties. Hit the source that hurts, darkened blue eyes, no hope left at this time, love is impossible when stepped on, walk across the zip wire of trauma, stay on or fall off this line.

Progression

Down to the darkened room, laying in my pit of thoughts. Streams flow to currents grow, over and over on the plain sheet. New beginnings, I hope so, finding the source, will I ever meet? Will watch how it goes. Council room, my medication will bloom, get back on the right path soon.

Fantasy or reality?

Sitting on the floor, blanked from reality, living in a place, can't be free. Holds me down, new generation, wrong sound. Be in that world, that world in my mind. Escape through daze, trapped for days, dreams seem real, or I want them to be. Fantasy or reality? Only I can see.

Hit me with words

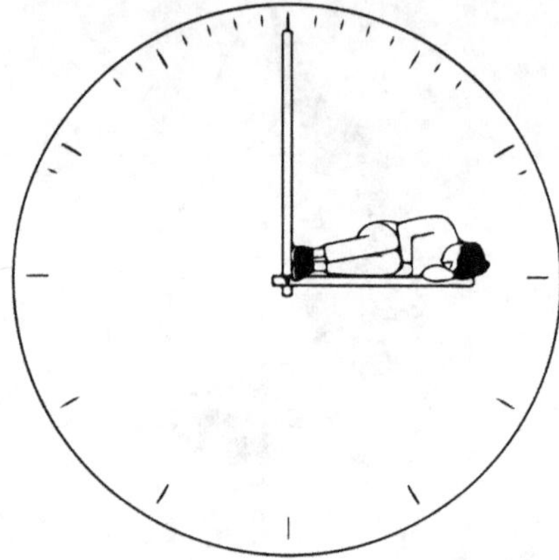

Importance? You don't know such thing, young kid, big world, lessons that shouldn't be learnt. Price and pay, tell me all day, care tough luck, I slept through your classes, all pain, I'm stuck. I needed you in my young mind, I let you go in my older mind.

My Hero

Together in this world, born and loved, through crying and hugs. Hardships and gaining, kept pushing through training. Give up, not an option, pick up, was the choice. Kindness and love, give others and give us. Hold my hand down the path, don't let go, need you always. Felt supported every time, through every year and every whine, I'm here, you're here, love you now and love you then, in the beginning and in the end.

Not the real me

Nerve unsettling, confidence is pending, only there whilst mind racing. Me I want to be, escaping will not set me free. Practice won't make perfect, nothing and nobody is, don't keep at it, will only effect.

Storm inside

Walk across, me, the sea and freedom. Sand between my toes, clouds once light but darkened each step, move faster before rain falls upon, get to the shore, before you're stuck once more, thunder louder, head paining, jump to the end, catch breath whilst laying.

See what should be seen

Time spent away, escape for another day, daze into the rippled cold river, stare at the blossoming pink flowers, migrate through nature, climb above the greens, shape the clouds, see what should be seen.

Father figure

Entered our home, first distant now close. Father figures failed, not you, made me have trust again, you're the one that hasn't bailed. Make us all happy, only our home when you're here. Confidence built, not shy behind hidden guilt. Thank you for being you, funny and a complete goof, ain't different from us all, we're all good at being fools. Fish down the line, swim faster, I know you'll appreciate that rhyme, won't give up on you, if you don't on us, keep that connection and forever that trust.

Best friend

Always there, in the shallows and darkest times of despair. Changed my life, helped me trust, family I'm blessed with, support forever, through all the must. Dominos and jokes, sense of humour won't ever be broke, my best friend is you, can never be replaced, even when your annoying humour gives me a slap in the face.

Hurricane

The hurricane of life, beautiful to see, hard to face, you keep pushing the wave, put it in its place, kindness and love, gets you right above, water currents fight, reaching beyond such great height, gorgeous inside and out, powerful all around, don't stop trying until you hit the ground, happiness brought to others, smiles blinding the shore, worth all the good, such heart with such pure.

Not the end

Everything else closed, pain opened, waterfalls have risen upon the skin surface, drowned. Broken down in sorrow, my dad and always will be, more supportive than the original. Kindness and love will keep you safe above. I'll keep holding your hand until we meet again, my best friends.